Kick start Your
Etsy POD Business:
A Step-by-Step Guide

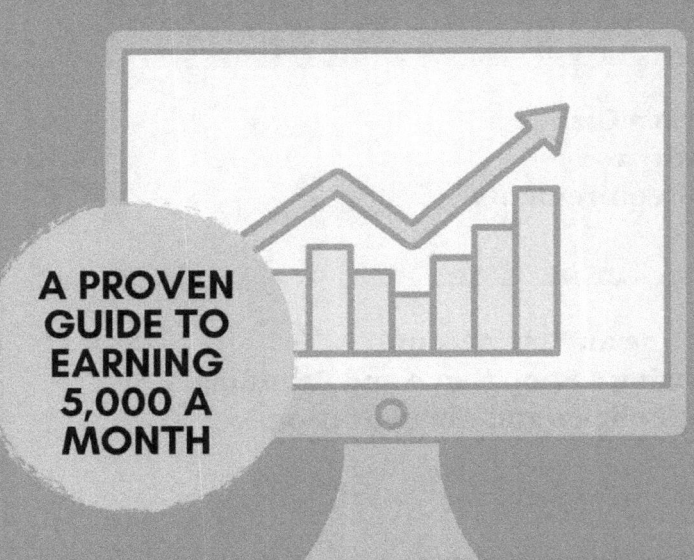

A PROVEN GUIDE TO EARNING 5,000 A MONTH

by Joao Nsita

Table of Contents

1. Introduction to Print on Demand

- What Is POD?
- Why Choose Etsy + Printify?
- Benefits and Challenges

2. Getting Started—Etsy & Printify Overview

- Etsy at a Glance
- Printify 101
- Key Requirements

3. Setting Up Your Etsy Shop

- Creating an Etsy Account
- Choosing a Shop Name and Branding
- Shop Policies and About Section

4. Connecting Etsy with Printify

- Printify Account Setup
- App Integration
- Syncing Settings

5. Designing Your First Product

- The Printify Mockup Generator
- Basic Design Principles
- Sourcing Artwork

6. Selecting Print Providers

- Working with Printify's Network
- Evaluating Quality and Costs
- Choosing International vs. Local Providers

7. Product Research & Market Validation

- Finding a Profitable Niche
- Analyzing Top Sellers
- Testing Demand

8. Branding Your Etsy Shop

- Crafting a Cohesive Identity
- Shop Sections & Categories
- Storytelling & Brand Voice

9. Listing Optimization & SEO

- Keyword Research
- Writing Titles & Tags
- Product Descriptions

10. Pricing Your Products

- Calculating Costs
- Profit Margins
- Promotions & Coupons

11. Managing Orders & Customer Service

- Order Fulfillment
- Tracking & Communication
- Handling Returns & Refunds

12. Launch Strategies

- Setting a Publication Date and Creating a Launch Plan
- Coordinating Pre-Orders or Early Reviews
- Building Excitement on Social Media and Email Lists
- Pricing Strategies for Launch

13. Building an Author Platform

- Importance of an Online Presence
- Engaging with Readers via Social Media
- Networking with Other Authors and Communities
- Using Author Branding to Stand Out

14. Marketing Tactics for POD Books

- Paid Advertising (Amazon Ads, Facebook Ads, BookBub)
- Organic Marketing (Content Marketing, Guest Blogging, Podcast Appearances)
- Strategies for Garnering Early Reviews
- Long-Term Marketing vs. Short Promotional Bursts

15. Leveraging Analytics and Sales Data

- Interpreting Sales Reports and Royalty Statements
- Tracking Key Performance Indicators (KPIs)
- Adjusting Marketing Efforts Based on Data
- Testing Different Price Points and Promotional Strategies

16. Expanding Beyond Amazon

- IngramSpark, Lulu, and Other POD Options
- Pros and Cons of Wide Distribution
- Pricing and Royalty Differences in Various Marketplaces

- Managing Multiple Distribution Channels

17. Handling Customer Feedback and Reviews

- Strategies for Encouraging Positive Reviews
- Dealing with Negative Feedback Professionally
- Using Feedback to Improve Future Editions
- Building Reader Loyalty Through Engagement

18. Scaling Your POD Business

- Publishing Additional Books or Related Products
- Collaborative Projects with Other Authors or Experts
- Creating Series or Brand Consistency Across Multiple Books
- Outsourcing Tasks to Grow Efficiently

19. Legal and Administrative Considerations

- Copyright Basics and ISBN Requirements
- Tax Obligations and Best Practices
- Intellectual Property and Plagiarism Concerns
- Protecting Yourself and Your Work

20. The Future of Your Print on Demand Journey

- Maintaining Momentum and Continuous Improvement
- Exploring New Book Formats
- Keeping Up with Industry Changes and Updates
- Final Words of Encouragement and Next Steps

21. Maximizing Traffic to Your Etsy Shop – 20 Proven Methods

- Leveraging SEO with Fresh Keywords
- Optimizing Product Photography

- Utilizing Pinterest Boards
- Collaborating with Influencers
- Running Targeted Etsy Ads

22. Social Media Marketing for Your POD Brand

- Choosing the Right Platforms
- Crafting Engaging Content
- Scheduling & Consistency
- Analytics & Adjustments

23. Collaboration & Partnerships

- Working with Fellow Creators
- Brand Partnerships
- Affiliate and Influencer Marketing

24. Expanding to Amazon – KDP and Merch by Amazon

- Deciding Your Approach
- Listing & Optimization
- Prime Benefits & Global Reach
- Challenges & Fees

25. Harnessing the Power of Shopify

- Why Shopify?
- Choosing POD Integrations
- Building a Professional Storefront
- Marketing & Apps

26. Building a Multi-Channel Brand

- Developing a Consistent Brand Identity
- Inventory & Listing Management
- Pricing Strategies
- Customer Experience

27. Cross-Selling, Upselling, and Bundling

- Product Bundles
- Upselling Techniques
- Customer Journey Maps
- Bundling for Different Seasons

28. Streamlining Fulfillment and Logistics

- Multi-Warehouse Solutions
- Automated Shipping & Tracking
- Quality Control
- Scaling Customer Service

29. Data-Driven Growth & Automation

- Analytics Tools
- Sales Funnel Optimization
- Setting Up Automation
- Continuous Improvement

30. Future Innovations and Trends in POD

- Sustainability and Eco-Friendly Products
- Emerging Marketing Channels
- Interactive & Personalized Products
- Long-Term Vision

31. Embracing the Journey from Day One

- A Fresh Beginning
- Setting Realistic Goals
- Building Confidence in Your Process

32. Pushing Through the Dip – Surviving the "No Results" Phase

- Understanding the Dip

- Strategies to Overcome Slow Periods
- Building Resilience

33. Reflecting on Your Why – Connecting with Your Core Purpose

- Clarifying Your Motivation
- Exercises to Reinforce Purpose
- Emotional Anchors

34. Mastering Self-Motivation – Overcoming the Urge to Quit

- Common Obstacles to Motivation
- Techniques to Boost Internal Drive
- Converting Setbacks into Opportunities

35. Celebrating Milestones – Turning Small Wins into Big Momentum

- Why Acknowledging Small Victories Matters
- Sustaining Energy Through Milestone Celebrations
- Engaging Supporters in Achievements

36. Deepening Your Creative Process – Tapping Into New Sources of Inspiration

- Finding Fresh Ideas
- Experimenting with New Techniques
- Sustaining Creative Growth

37. Mastering the Art of Design Trends

- Staying Ahead with Popular Design Styles
- Researching Visual Preferences Across Niches
- Tools and Techniques for Creating Trend-Forward Designs

38. Customer Persona Development

- Understanding Your Target Audience
- Crafting Detailed Customer Personas
- Using Personas to Refine Marketing Strategies

39. Crafting the Perfect Product Bundle

- Types of Bundles and Their Benefits
- Pricing Strategies for Bundles
- Promoting Bundles Effectively

40. Evolving with Market Shifts and Innovation

- Identifying Market Trends and Consumer Behavior
- Adapting to Emerging POD Niches
- Innovating Within Your Brand Identity

41. Innovative Marketing Beyond the Basics

- Exploring Unconventional Marketing Channels
- Leveraging Interactive Content for Engagement
- Experimenting with New Ad Formats

42. The Psychology of Pricing

- How Pricing Affects Consumer Behavior
- Psychological Pricing Strategies
- Testing and Optimizing Price Points

43. Nurturing a Loyal Community for Long-Term Growth

- Building Relationships Through Engagement
- Rewarding Loyalty with Exclusive Perks
- Encouraging Word-of-Mouth Advocacy

44. Sustainable Practices in POD

- Incorporating Eco-Friendly Products and Packaging
- Marketing Sustainability to Conscious Consumers
- Reducing Waste in Production Processes

45. Future-Proofing Your Etsy POD Business

- Diversifying Revenue Streams
- Preparing for Technological Changes
- Building a Resilient Business Model

46. Global Expansion and Localization

- Adapting Products for International Markets
- Navigating Shipping and Tax Regulations Globally
- Creating Multilingual Listings for Localization

Next Steps and Implementation

1. Finalize Your Topic
2. Create a Writing Schedule
3. Budget and Resources
4. Gather Tools and Accounts
5. Plan Your Launch

A Note of Gratitude

Chapter 1: Introduction to Print on Demand

Welcome to the world of print on demand, a business model that makes it possible for creative entrepreneurs and small business owners to sell custom-designed products without having to manage inventory or invest in expensive equipment. Whether you're an artist, designer, or simply have an eye for good aesthetics, print on demand can be an excellent way to turn your ideas into tangible items that customers can enjoy around the world.

What Is POD?

Print on Demand (POD) is a fulfillment method in which items—such as T-shirts, mugs, tote bags, phone cases, and more—are produced only after a customer places an order. Rather than stocking a large inventory, you partner with a printing supplier (like Printify) that custom-prints each product on your behalf. Once an order is made, the design is printed, packaged, and shipped directly to your customer. This model reduces upfront costs and virtually eliminates the risk of unsold merchandise.

By leveraging POD, you can:

- **Focus on creative work** rather than inventory management.
- **Save on storage space** since products are only printed as needed.
- **Expand your product line** quickly by testing new designs without large investments.

Why Choose Etsy + Printify?

When it comes to starting a POD business, **Etsy** and **Printify** offer a particularly powerful combination:

1. **Etsy's Global Marketplace**
   Etsy is a well-known online marketplace where shoppers look specifically for unique, handcrafted, or custom products. Its large and diverse audience is already primed to appreciate creative, personalized, or niche designs, giving you a higher chance of finding customers who value originality.
2. **Printify's Print Network**
   Printify simplifies the production and fulfillment process. You can easily upload your artwork or designs, select from numerous product options, and then integrate your listings seamlessly into your Etsy shop. Printify works with a global network of production partners, so you can cater to customers around the world without worrying about shipping logistics or setting up your own print facility.
3. **Seamless Integration**
   With just a few clicks, Etsy and Printify can be synced. This setup ensures that orders placed on Etsy get automatically sent to Printify, which prints and ships them, saving you time and letting you focus on branding, marketing, and creating new designs.

Benefits and Challenges

Benefits

- **Low Startup Costs:** You don't have to purchase inventory or expensive equipment. Your major investment is your time and creativity.
- **Global Reach:** Etsy has an international audience, and Printify has printing partners worldwide, letting you sell internationally without having to handle overseas shipping directly.
- **Creative Freedom:** POD allows you to experiment with designs and product types. You can quickly add new listings or remove underperforming products.

Challenges

- **Competition:** Because it's relatively easy to open an Etsy shop and start a POD business, standing out can be difficult. You'll need a strategy for branding, unique designs, and marketing to attract customers.
- **Shipping Times & Costs:** While Printify connects you to worldwide print providers, production and shipping times can vary. Managing customer expectations about delivery windows is crucial.
- **Profit Margins:** You must carefully price your products to ensure profitability after manufacturing, shipping, and marketplace fees.

Chapter 2: Getting Started—Etsy & Printify Overview

When launching a print-on-demand (POD) business, two platforms you'll likely hear about are **Etsy** and **Printify**. Each plays a distinct role in helping you reach customers and efficiently fulfill orders. In this chapter, we'll explore why Etsy is ideal for creative entrepreneurs, how Printify works, and the key requirements you should have in place before you open your shop.

Etsy at a Glance

- **Brief History**
  Launched in 2005, Etsy set out to be a marketplace primarily for handmade, vintage, and unique items. Over time, it has grown into a global platform where independent makers and small businesses connect with customers who appreciate originality, craft, and personal touch.
- **Demographics**
  Etsy attracts a wide spectrum of shoppers—from collectors of artistic pieces to those searching for personalized gifts. The site's community-based ethos and focus on creativity make it particularly suitable for entrepreneurs offering custom-designed goods.
- **Why Etsy Is Great for Creative Entrepreneurs**
  - **Built-in Audience:** Shoppers come to Etsy looking for unique or personalized products.
  - **User-Friendly Interface:** Setting up a shop is relatively straightforward, with intuitive tools for listing products and managing orders.
  - **Community & Support:** Etsy offers seller handbooks, forums, and articles to help you grow and optimize your shop.

Printify 101

- **What Is Printify?**
  Printify is a print-on-demand platform that connects you with a global network of print providers. When a customer orders a product, Printify handles the printing and ships it directly to the buyer.
- **E-Commerce Integrations**
  Printify integrates seamlessly with various online storefronts like Shopify, WooCommerce, and **Etsy**. This means you can create your designs in Printify, push them to your Etsy shop, and let the two platforms handle order processing and fulfillment behind the scenes.
- **Focus on Etsy Integration**
  For this guide, we'll highlight how to link Printify with Etsy so that any orders you receive on Etsy are automatically routed to the print provider. You won't have to manually coordinate shipping or production.

Key Requirements

- **Payment Methods**
  Before you list products, decide how you'll pay for production costs through Printify (credit card, PayPal, etc.). Etsy also requires bank information to deposit your earnings and to charge fees.
- **Business Information**
  Depending on your location, you may need a business license, tax ID, or other documentation. While Etsy doesn't always require these upfront, it's wise to understand your local regulations before selling.
- **Initial Steps Before Opening**
  1. Research successful Etsy shops in your niche.

2. Outline the types of designs or products you'll create.
3. Gather essential branding assets (logo, banner images) or plan to create them soon.

Once these preliminary tasks are done, you'll be ready to open an Etsy shop and integrate it with Printify.

Chapter 3: Setting Up Your Etsy Shop

Now that you're familiar with Etsy's environment and how Printify will fit into your plan, it's time to **officially open your Etsy shop**. In this chapter, we'll walk you through creating an account, choosing a memorable name, and setting up your shop policies—key steps to making a strong first impression on potential customers.

Creating an Etsy Account

1. **Sign Up**
   Go to Etsy's homepage and click on the "Sign in" or "Register" button. Provide the required information, such as your email and a secure password.
2. **Open Your Shop**
   Once you're logged in, choose "Sell on Etsy" and follow the prompts to start the setup process. You'll be asked about your country, currency preferences, and other basic details.
3. **Banking & Tax Info**
   Etsy requires information for depositing your sales income. Provide the necessary bank or PayPal details, along with any tax ID if required in your region.
4. **Shop Preferences**
   Set your shop language, the currency you'll list prices in, and the country you operate from. These preferences help Etsy display accurate information to your potential buyers.

Choosing a Shop Name and Branding

- **Memorable Shop Name**
  Pick something that reflects your niche or brand personality. Keep it concise, easy to spell, and available (Etsy will notify you if a name is already taken).
- **Visual Branding**
  Upload a banner or cover photo that showcases your style, and consider adding a logo for a professional appearance. Consistent fonts, colors, and imagery across your shop, social media, and packaging can strengthen brand recognition.

Shop Policies and About Section

- **Policies**
  Clearly outline your shipping policies, processing times, returns, and exchanges. Transparent policies build trust and reduce confusion.
- **About Section**
  Share your story—why you started this shop, what inspires your designs, and what customers can expect from your brand. This personal touch can help shoppers connect with you on a deeper level.

Chapter 4: Connecting Etsy with Printify

With your Etsy shop live, the next step is to **link Printify to Etsy** so you can easily create and manage print-on-demand listings. By doing so, any order placed on Etsy will be automatically transmitted to Printify, streamlining the entire production and fulfillment process.

Printify Account Setup

1. **Sign Up for Printify**
   Go to the Printify website and create a free account using your email address, Google account, or other sign-in method.
2. **Enter Billing Details**
   Add a payment method (credit card, PayPal, etc.) to cover production and shipping costs whenever orders come in. You can update or change this method at any time.
3. **Familiarize Yourself with the Dashboard**
   Explore the Printify dashboard to see where you'll manage products, orders, and your connected online stores.

App Integration

1. **Access the "My Stores" Tab**
   Once logged into Printify, navigate to "My Stores."
2. **Connect Your Etsy Shop**
   Click "Add a New Store" or "Connect" and select Etsy. You'll be prompted to sign in to your Etsy account (if you aren't already). Grant Printify permission to access your shop.

3. **Authorize Integration**
   Follow the on-screen instructions. Etsy may ask you to confirm that you trust Printify to publish and manage listings.

This process typically only takes a few minutes. If you run into issues, check Printify's help center or Etsy's support resources for troubleshooting guides.

Syncing Settings

- **Product Listings**
  Once your store is connected, you can create new products or sync existing ones. Design your product in Printify, choose your printing partner, and select "Publish" to send it to Etsy as a draft or active listing.
- **Shipping Profiles**
  Printify can automatically generate shipping profiles, or you can customize your own in Etsy. Ensure the shipping costs and estimated delivery times are accurate for each product type.
- **Order Handling**
  When a customer orders from your Etsy shop, Printify receives the order details (size, color, address) and starts production. Keep an eye on orders in both Etsy and Printify dashboards to stay informed about their status.

Chapter 5: Designing Your First Product

When you're ready to create your first print-on-demand (POD) product, you'll likely be excited—this is where your brand's creativity truly begins to shine. By leveraging Printify's tools and a few basic design principles, you can bring your ideas to life with minimal hassle.

The Printify Mockup Generator

One of Printify's key strengths is its user-friendly **Mockup Generator**. Here's how to make the most of it:

1. **Choose Your Product Variant**
   Printify offers a variety of product categories—T-shirts, hoodies, mugs, tote bags, phone cases, and more. Select a product that aligns with your brand and audience preferences.
2. **Upload Your Design**
   Once you've chosen a product, upload your artwork in a compatible file format (PNG or JPEG). Place the image on the product, adjusting size and position as needed.
3. **Preview & Save**
   The mockup generator provides a 2D preview (and sometimes 3D previews) of how your final product will look. Make any necessary tweaks, then save your design.

Basic Design Principles

Whether you're a professional designer or new to the process, understanding **basic design principles** can help ensure your products look polished:

- **File Formats:** Generally, **PNG** files with a transparent background are ideal for T-shirts and other apparel. JPEGs can work for full-bleed prints or photo-based designs.
- **Resolution:** Aim for **300 DPI** (dots per inch) or higher to prevent pixelation in the final print.
- **Color Profiles (RGB vs. CMYK):** While printing is technically done in CMYK, Printify and many POD providers often accept artwork in RGB format. If you're particular about color accuracy, consider converting your designs to CMYK before uploading—but always check the product specs for best results.

Sourcing Artwork

You have multiple options when it comes to creating or obtaining designs:

- **DIY Tools:** Platforms like **Canva**, **Adobe Photoshop**, or **Illustrator** make it easier than ever to design your own graphics. Canva's drag-and-drop interface is great for beginners, while Photoshop or Illustrator provide more advanced capabilities.
- **Hiring Freelancers:** If you're not confident in your design skills or want a distinctive look, consider hiring a freelance graphic designer from sites like **Fiverr** or **Upwork**. Provide a clear brief and examples to ensure you get designs that match your brand's style.

Chapter 6: Selecting Print Providers

Picking the right print provider is essential to balancing cost, quality, and customer satisfaction. With Printify, you gain access to a global network of production facilities, but you'll still need to decide which one best meets your needs for each product type.

Working with Printify's Network

Printify acts as a hub connecting you to a variety of print partners worldwide. You can:

- **Compare Providers**: Each provider has a rating, location, shipping times, and customer reviews.
- **Select for Each Product**: You can choose different providers for T-shirts versus mugs, for example, based on their specialties or pricing.
- **Automated Fulfillment**: Once you set your preferred provider for a listing, Printify automatically routes orders to that facility.

Evaluating Quality and Costs

Balancing affordability with top-notch quality can be tricky. Consider:

- **Print Costs and Shipping Fees**: Look at the base price of a product plus the shipping cost. Some providers might offer a lower print cost but higher shipping, so calculate your total expense.
- **Production Times**: Providers have varying turnaround times. If your customers expect quick delivery, choose a faster supplier—especially for holiday or special-event items.
- **Samples and Reviews**: Order samples from different providers to check print clarity, fabric quality, or color

accuracy. Customer reviews and feedback in Printify can also guide your decision.

Choosing International vs. Local Providers

- **Shipping Times**: A local print facility can speed up delivery and reduce shipping costs for nearby customers, but if you sell globally, you may want to choose providers in multiple regions.
- **Customer Satisfaction**: Faster shipping times typically translate into happier buyers. However, if you're catering to an international market, you might need to partner with multiple print hubs for consistency.
- **Returns and Exchanges**: Coordinating returns to international providers can be costlier and more complicated. Ensure you outline a clear return policy in your Etsy shop to manage expectations.

Chapter 7: Product Research & Market Validation

Creating designs is only half the battle; ensuring there's demand for them is crucial. Conducting market research helps you refine product ideas, identify profitable niches, and gauge how your audience might react.

Finding a Profitable Niche

- **Etsy Search & Trends**: Check the Etsy search bar for autocomplete suggestions, explore trending keywords, and see what customers are actively looking for.
- **Competitor Analysis**: Browse existing shops in the categories you're interested in. Look at their best-selling products and identify gaps you could fill with a unique twist.
- **Social Media & Community Groups**: Places like Pinterest, Instagram, or niche Facebook groups can inspire popular motifs, trending memes, or color palettes that might resonate with your target audience.

Analyzing Top Sellers

Observing successful sellers on Etsy (and potentially on other platforms) can give you insights into:

- **Design Styles**: Are minimalist designs trending, or do vibrant, detailed illustrations sell better in your niche?
- **Product Types**: T-shirts, phone cases, tote bags—each product has different margins and market saturation.
- **Pricing Strategies**: Identify the average price range for popular items and how it correlates with brand positioning (budget vs. premium).

Testing Demand

Before going all-in on any single idea:

1. **List a Few Items First**: Add a small collection of products to gauge customer interest.
2. **Gather Feedback**: Monitor views, favorites, sales, and customer messages to see how well your items resonate.
3. **Refine or Expand**: If certain products sell well, consider adding variations or related designs. If you're not getting the traction you hoped for, adjust your designs or try a different approach.

Chapter 8: Branding Your Etsy Shop

Establishing a strong, consistent brand is one of the best ways to set yourself apart on Etsy. Your brand identity not only reflects your style but also communicates to potential buyers what they can expect from your products and service.

Crafting a Cohesive Identity

- **Logos & Color Palettes**
  Your logo is often the first visual cue customers see. Make sure it's clean, memorable, and representative of your niche. Select two or three colors that complement each other and reflect your brand's personality (e.g., warm and vibrant for a fun brand, soft and muted for a minimalist brand).
- **Banner Images**
  Etsy allows you to upload a shop banner or cover photo. Use this space to showcase your best-selling items, display your brand aesthetic, or highlight a seasonal promotion. A cohesive banner helps tie your branding together.
- **Consistency Across Platforms**
  If you have social media accounts, use the same logo and color scheme there. Consistency across all channels builds brand recognition and trust.

Shop Sections & Categories

- **Organizing Products**
  Group products into sections (e.g., T-shirts, Mugs, Tote Bags) to help customers quickly find what they're looking for. Keep section names intuitive and relevant.
- **Navigational Ease**
  A well-organized shop reduces customer frustration and increases the likelihood of sales. If you offer multiple types of designs or themes, consider sub-categories (e.g., "Funny Mugs," "Inspirational Mugs").

- **Updating Regularly**
  As you add or remove product lines, update your shop sections so customers always have a clear view of your current offerings.

Storytelling & Brand Voice

- **Authentic Messaging**
  Share the inspiration behind your designs and how you got started. Customers often value the story as much as the product itself.
- **Brand Voice**
  Decide how you want to talk to your audience—friendly, playful, professional, whimsical? Use this tone consistently in product descriptions, announcements, and social media posts.
- **Connecting with Customers**
  Encourage buyers to become part of your journey. You can share behind-the-scenes content, sketches, or photos that highlight the process of creating your designs.

Chapter 9: Listing Optimization & SEO

With a cohesive brand in place, it's time to optimize your listings for discoverability. Understanding how Etsy's search algorithm works will help you reach more potential buyers and increase sales.

Keyword Research

- **Etsy Search Bar**
  Start typing keywords related to your products (e.g., "funny cat mug") to see what Etsy suggests. These suggestions are popular customer searches.
- **Third-Party Tools**
  Platforms like **eRank** or **Marmalead** analyze real-time data on trending keywords, search volume, and competition levels.
- **Competitive Analysis**
  Check out successful listings in your niche. Identify common keywords they use, and consider how you might adapt them for your own products.

Writing Titles & Tags

- **Balancing Readability with SEO**
  Include relevant keywords in your title, but keep it understandable and appealing to human readers. Avoid keyword stuffing, as it can look spammy.
- **Strategic Tagging**
  Etsy allows up to 13 tags per listing. Use all of them wisely. Combine single words and phrases to capture multiple search queries (e.g., "cat mug," "funny gift," "cat lover gift").
- **Avoid Redundancy**
  If your title already contains "funny cat mug," you don't necessarily need to repeat the exact phrase in your tags. You can vary them slightly to capture similar searches.

Product Descriptions

- **Highlight Features & Care Instructions**
  Provide essential details like materials used, sizing, and

care guidelines (e.g., machine-wash cold for T-shirts). This reduces the chance of returns and increases customer satisfaction.
- **Brand Story Integration**
A short paragraph on why this design is special or how it ties into your brand's ethos can make your listing more memorable.
- **Call to Action**
Encourage shoppers to add items to their cart, explore related listings in your shop, or reach out with any questions.

Chapter 10: Pricing Your Products

Setting the right price can make or break your print-on-demand venture. You need to cover costs, make a profit, and ensure the price point aligns with your brand and market expectations.

Calculating Costs

- **Base Cost**
  Check how much each item costs to produce via Printify (including variations in color or size).
- **Shipping & Etsy Fees**
  Consider Printify's shipping fees, plus Etsy's listing fee ($0.20 per listing) and transaction fee (a percentage of the sale). Don't forget about payment processing fees if you're using Etsy Payments or PayPal.
- **Taxes**
  Depending on your location, you may owe sales tax or VAT. Consult a tax professional to make sure you set aside the correct amount.

Profit Margins

- **Markup Strategies**
  A common approach is to aim for a markup of 2x or 3x the cost of goods. However, this depends on your niche and the perceived value of your brand.
- **Testing & Adjusting**
  List your items at a price you believe is fair. If they sell quickly, you might raise the price slightly. If they don't, consider if the price or the product presentation needs tweaking.

Promotions & Coupons

- **When to Offer Discounts**
  Running a sale can boost visibility and attract

bargain-hunting customers. Consider holiday or seasonal promotions for maximum impact.

- **Types of Discounts**
  You can offer percentage off, free shipping, or buy-one-get-one deals. Evaluate which approach is most enticing to your audience.
- **Coupon Codes**
  Reward repeat customers or newsletter subscribers by sending them exclusive coupon codes. This can help build loyalty and encourage future purchases.

Chapter 11: Managing Orders & Customer Service

Even the most beautifully designed store won't succeed without efficient order management and top-notch customer service. Luckily, Etsy and Printify handle much of the heavy lifting for you, but you'll still play a crucial role in ensuring a smooth experience.

Order Fulfillment

- **Automatic Processing**
  When a customer places an order on Etsy, it's automatically sent to Printify if you've integrated your store correctly. The print provider will then produce and ship the item directly to your buyer.
- **Monitoring Orders**
  Check the status of orders in both Etsy and Printify dashboards. This helps you identify and address any issues (e.g., out-of-stock items) promptly.

Tracking & Communication

- **Shipping Notifications**
  Etsy will send buyers an automated shipping notification. However, it's good practice to occasionally send a personal message, thanking them for their purchase.
- **Delays & Updates**
  If production or shipping takes longer than anticipated, keep your customer informed. Prompt, transparent communication often prevents negative reviews.

Handling Returns & Refunds

- **Clear Policies**
  Outline how you handle returns, exchanges, and refunds in your shop's policy section. This includes whether

customers need to pay for return shipping and how many days they have to initiate a return.
- **Best Practices**
  - **Stay Professional & Empathetic:** Even if a customer is upset, respond politely and work towards a fair resolution.
  - **Offer Solutions:** Depending on the situation, this might mean a replacement product, a partial refund, or store credit.
  - **Protect Your Reputation:** Excellent customer service can lead to positive reviews and repeat business, which is crucial on Etsy.

Chapter 12: Launch Strategies

Once you've put time and effort into writing and preparing your print-on-demand book, you'll want to ensure its release makes a splash. A carefully organized **launch strategy** can significantly boost initial sales, garner early reviews, and help you stand out in a crowded marketplace.

Setting a Publication Date and Creating a Launch Plan

- **Choosing the Right Date**
  Consider any relevant holidays, seasonal trends, or events. For example, if your book covers a Valentine's Day topic, plan your launch a few weeks before February 14.
- **Countdown & Teasers**
  Plan backward from your chosen release date. Create a timeline with tasks such as cover reveals, social media teasers, email announcements, and final proof checks.
- **Milestones & Checklists**
  Break your launch plan into milestones—finalizing the manuscript, approving proofs, scheduling promotional content—so you don't miss any critical steps.

Coordinating Pre-Orders or Early Reviews

- **Advantages of Pre-Orders**
  Platforms like Amazon KDP allow readers to pre-order your book. Pre-orders help build momentum, and all sales count toward your release-day rank, giving you a higher visibility boost.
- **Securing Early Reviews**
  Ask beta readers, trusted colleagues, or members of your

author community to provide feedback and reviews before the official launch date. Early reviews can lend credibility and encourage hesitant buyers.
- **Review Copies**
Consider sending out advance reader copies (ARCs) to influencers, bloggers, or journalists who might endorse or feature your book.

Building Excitement on Social Media and Email Lists

- **Social Media Hype**
Share behind-the-scenes snippets on Instagram, Facebook, TikTok, or your preferred platforms. Tease the cover design, table of contents, or a short excerpt to build curiosity.
- **Email Newsletters**
Send out regular updates to your mailing list, counting down to launch day. Offer exclusive sneak peeks or an early-bird discount code for loyal subscribers.
- **Collaborations & Giveaways**
Team up with fellow authors or complementary businesses. Host a giveaway where participants can win a free copy of your book or related merchandise.

Pricing Strategies for Launch

- **Introductory Pricing**
Some authors price their book slightly lower for the first week or two to incentivize early buyers and encourage word-of-mouth.
- **Limited-Time Deals**
Consider offering a short-term discount or bundle deal (e.g., buy the paperback and get the ebook free). Promoting a sense of urgency can drive sales.
- **Long-Term Pricing**
After launch, reassess your price based on feedback and

sales data. Adjust if you find your target audience is willing to pay more (or less) for your book.

Chapter 13: Building an Author Platform

An **author platform** represents your ability to reach a loyal audience and influence potential readers. It combines your online presence, professional connections, and personal brand—essential for long-term success in the print-on-demand world.

Importance of an Online Presence (Website, Blog)

- **Central Hub**
  A professional website or blog acts as your online home base. Readers can find information about your books, sign up for newsletters, and stay up-to-date on your latest news.
- **SEO Benefits**
  Regularly updating your blog with fresh content (e.g., writing tips, personal insights, book recommendations) can help you rank higher in search engine results, attracting organic traffic.
- **Credibility & Professionalism**
  A well-designed site signals to readers that you take your writing career seriously, building trust in your brand.

Engaging with Readers via Social Media and Newsletters

- **Choose the Right Channels**
  Focus on platforms where your target audience is most active. Writers of romance might thrive on TikTok or Instagram, while business authors may prefer LinkedIn or Twitter.
- **Consistency & Authenticity**
  Post consistently, but prioritize quality over quantity. Share personal anecdotes, writing insights, or life experiences that resonate with your readership.
- **Email Newsletters**
  Email lists offer direct communication with your audience.

Use newsletters to announce new releases, highlight behind-the-scenes content, and reward loyal subscribers with exclusive deals.

Networking with Other Authors and Communities

- **Author Collaborations**
  Guest posts, anthologies, co-hosted webinars—teaming up with fellow authors can expand your reach to new audiences.
- **Writing Communities**
  Join local writer groups, online forums, or Facebook groups. Giving and receiving support fosters relationships and can lead to valuable connections down the road.
- **Events & Workshops**
  Attending book fairs, writers' conferences, or virtual seminars can help you sharpen your craft and meet potential collaborators or fans.

Using Author Branding to Stand Out

- **Consistent Visual Identity**
  Use the same headshot, logo, colors, or font styles across your website, social media profiles, and promotional materials.
- **Unified Messaging**
  Develop a tagline or mission statement that summarizes what readers can expect from your work—whether it's thrilling mysteries or heartfelt self-help.
- **Public Persona**
  Decide how personal you want to get. Some authors focus strictly on their writing, while others share personal stories to build deeper connections.

Chapter 14: Marketing Tactics for POD Books

Even with an author platform and a well-executed launch, ongoing **marketing efforts** will keep your book in the spotlight. Think of marketing as a long-term conversation rather than a one-time push.

Paid Advertising (Amazon Ads, Facebook Ads, BookBub)

- **Amazon Ads**
  Target specific keywords or interests on Amazon. Ads can be cost-effective if you optimize keywords and continuously monitor performance.
- **Facebook & Instagram Ads**
  Leverage demographic targeting to reach potential readers. Test different ad creatives, headlines, and audiences to find what works best.
- **BookBub Promotions**
  BookBub's large subscriber base makes it a powerful platform for boosting visibility, especially if you manage to secure a featured deal. However, competition and costs can be high.

Organic Marketing (Content Marketing, Guest Blogging, Podcast Appearances)

- **Content Marketing**
  Write articles or blog posts related to your book's theme. Offer helpful tips or unique insights that position you as an expert in your genre.
- **Guest Blogging**
  Pitch articles to popular blogs or magazines in your niche. This not only builds credibility but also introduces your work to a new audience.

- **Podcast Interviews**
  Podcasts looking for expert guests or storytellers can be a great way to reach engaged listeners. Share compelling anecdotes, writing tips, or personal experiences that tie back to your book.

Strategies for Garnering Early Reviews and Social Proof

- **ARC (Advance Reader Copy) Teams**
  Provide a free copy in exchange for an honest review around launch time. This can help establish initial credibility.
- **Review Swaps**
  While some authors engage in mutual review swaps, proceed with caution to maintain authenticity and follow platform guidelines.
- **Engage Readers**
  Encourage readers to share photos of your book on social media or to recommend it to friends. Positive word-of-mouth can be incredibly powerful.

Long-Term Marketing vs. Short Promotional Bursts

- **Consistent Visibility**
  Rather than relying on short bursts of intense promotion, plan a regular schedule for marketing efforts—blog posts, social media updates, giveaways, etc.
- **Evergreen Content**
  Focus on producing content that remains relevant over time. This helps draw steady traffic to your book even months or years after its launch.
- **Re-Launching & Seasonal Campaigns**
  Periodically refresh your marketing, especially if your book ties into a particular season or current event. Consider "re-launches" to re-energize sales.

Chapter 15: Leveraging Analytics and Sales Data

After launching and running marketing campaigns, **data** becomes your best ally. Monitoring your sales figures and reader engagement helps you tweak strategies to maximize results.

Interpreting Sales Reports and Royalty Statements

- **Platform Dashboards**
  Amazon KDP, IngramSpark, and other POD platforms provide real-time or regular sales updates. Track daily, weekly, or monthly performance.
- **Units Sold vs. Royalty Earnings**
  Note that each sale may yield a different royalty based on format (eBook vs. paperback), territory (U.S., UK, etc.), and price.
- **Trends Over Time**
  Look for patterns, such as sales spikes during promotions or dips when marketing activities paused.

Tracking Key Performance Indicators (KPIs)

- **Conversion Rate**
  The percentage of people who buy your book after seeing your ad or product page. Aim to improve this with better descriptions, covers, or blurbs.
- **Cost Per Click (CPC)**
  For paid ads, monitor how much you're spending per click and compare it against your revenue.
- **Return on Investment (ROI)**
  Assess the total cost of advertising, design, or marketing services and compare to the profit generated.

Adjusting Marketing Efforts Based on Data

- **Split Testing**
  Experiment with different book covers, ad creatives, price points, or product descriptions. Use the results to refine your approach.
- **Scaling Successful Tactics**
  If one social media ad is performing well, increase the budget. If a certain podcast interview drove significant sales, seek out similar audiences.
- **Cutting Underperforming Channels**
  Don't be afraid to drop tactics that aren't yielding results. Reallocate resources to more profitable endeavors.

Testing Different Price Points and Promotional Strategies

- **Seasonal & Limited-Time Discounts**
  Occasional price drops, free promotions, or giveaways can boost visibility and net new readers who might become loyal fans.
- **Bundling & Cross-Promotions**
  If you have multiple titles or related products, bundle them for a special offer. Cross-promote with authors in the same genre for mutual benefit.
- **Ongoing Analysis**
  Periodically revisit your pricing and promotional strategies. As your audience grows or the market changes, your pricing may need to evolve.

Chapter 16: Expanding Beyond Amazon

Once you've gotten comfortable with Amazon KDP and learned the ropes of publishing on the platform, you might be ready to take the next step: **expanding beyond Amazon**. Distributing your book through multiple channels can help you reach a wider audience, increase your earning potential, and establish a broader presence in the publishing world.

IngramSpark, Lulu, and Other POD Options

- **IngramSpark**
  One of the most popular alternatives to Amazon KDP. It offers a vast distribution network, including bookstores and libraries, but setup and print costs can be higher compared to some competitors.
- **Lulu**
  Lulu focuses on print-on-demand services for multiple formats (paperback, hardcover, photo books). It's known for its user-friendly interface, although it may have less reach than IngramSpark or Amazon.
- **Other POD Platforms**
  Smaller or more specialized companies may cater to specific types of books (e.g., coloring books, photography books) or unique binding options. Research each platform's fees and audience to determine if it suits your needs.

Pros and Cons of Wide Distribution

- **Pros**
  - **Increased Visibility**: By having your book on multiple platforms, you tap into a variety of reader bases.

- **Retail & Library Access**: IngramSpark, for instance, can make your title available for purchase in physical bookstores and libraries.
- **Diverse Revenue Streams**: If one marketplace slows, your book can continue performing on other platforms.

- **Cons**
  - **Complex Management**: Handling multiple dashboards, royalty reports, and distribution terms can be time-consuming.
  - **Higher Setup Costs**: Some platforms charge fees for listing, revisions, or ISBNs.
  - **Marketing Challenges**: Promoting your book across several platforms may require more effort and tailored strategies.

Pricing and Royalty Differences in Various Marketplaces

- **Platform Fees**
  Some POD platforms (like IngramSpark) charge setup fees or revision fees. Factor these into your budget.
- **Royalties**
  The royalty structure can differ significantly between Amazon KDP, IngramSpark, Lulu, etc. Review each platform's royalty rates, print costs, and retail discounts to understand your potential earnings.
- **Global Pricing**
  If you choose global distribution, you may need separate prices for regions like Europe, Canada, Australia, or the UK. Keep an eye on currency exchange rates and local taxes.

Managing Multiple Distribution Channels

- **Consolidated Tracking**
  Use spreadsheets or publishing-management software to keep track of which formats (paperback, hardcover, ebook)

are listed on which platforms, along with pricing and royalty rates.
- **Version Control**
  When updating your book (e.g., correcting typos or changing the cover), ensure all platforms receive the same revision to keep your editions consistent.
- **Strategic Focus**
  You don't necessarily need to distribute everywhere. Focus on a handful of key platforms that align best with your target audience and budget.

Chapter 17: Handling Customer Feedback and Reviews

Reviews are the lifeblood of a successful print-on-demand book. Positive feedback fosters trust and encourages new readers to give your work a chance, while negative reviews—when handled gracefully—can offer valuable insights for improvement.

Strategies for Encouraging Positive Reviews

- **Polite Requests**
  At the end of your book, include a gentle call-to-action asking readers to leave a review. Many readers are happy to do so but might need a reminder.
- **Email Follow-Up**
  If you have a mailing list, send a post-purchase follow-up thanking your readers and politely asking for feedback.
- **ARC Readers & Launch Teams**
  Recruit a group of dedicated readers to receive an Advance Reader Copy (ARC) in exchange for an honest review. Ensure this process complies with platform guidelines.

Dealing with Negative Feedback Professionally

- **Listen and Learn**
  Some negative reviews may raise legitimate points about plot holes, formatting issues, or unclear writing. Use these critiques to make future improvements.
- **Stay Professional**
  Resist the urge to argue with a negative reviewer publicly. Respond politely if you must, but remember that potential readers will judge your professionalism as much as your book's content.
- **Avoid 'Review Wars'**
  If someone leaves a harsh critique, focus on constructive

takeaways. Engaging in heated back-and-forth rarely wins you favor with potential customers.

Using Feedback to Improve Future Editions

- **Iterative Updates**
  POD platforms allow you to upload revised files. Correct typos, improve sections, or redesign covers based on consistent feedback.
- **Acknowledging Reviewer Input**
  If a recurring complaint emerges (e.g., grammar issues), address it promptly, and consider a professional editor for your next edition.
- **Building a Better Book**
  Over time, your readers can help shape a more polished, compelling version of your work—one that garners better reviews and sales.

Building Reader Loyalty Through Engagement

- **Social Media Interaction**
  Reply to messages, comments, and mentions. Show genuine appreciation for your readers' support.
- **Exclusive Content**
  Offer bonus chapters, short stories, or behind-the-scenes peeks to loyal fans. This fosters a sense of community and keeps readers invested in your work.
- **Reader-Centric Approach**
  Readers who feel valued and heard are more likely to recommend your book to friends, post positive reviews, and become repeat customers.

Chapter 18: Scaling Your POD Business

Once you've established a successful book (or a few), you may find yourself itching to do more. **Scaling your POD business** can mean increasing the scope of your product offerings, collaborating with other creatives, or streamlining your processes to free up time for new projects.

Publishing Additional Books or Related Products

- **Diversify Your Catalog**
  If you've published one genre or topic, consider branching out into adjacent niches. Nonfiction authors might add workbooks or journals; fiction authors might launch spinoffs or sequels.
- **Merchandise & Swag**
  Use the power of POD to create branded merchandise (e.g., T-shirts, mugs, tote bags) that tie into your book's theme or characters.
- **Build Author Prestige**
  A larger catalog can make you more discoverable. Readers who enjoy one book are likely to explore your other titles.

Collaborative Projects with Other Authors or Experts

- **Co-Authored Books**
  Team up with a writer who complements your style or expertise. This can open up both of your audiences to each other's work.
- **Anthologies**
  Contribute short stories or chapters to anthologies, or publish your own anthology with multiple authors, each bringing a unique perspective.
- **Events & Workshops**
  Partner with authors, editors, or marketers for webinars,

virtual summits, or live events that draw in potential readers.

Creating Series or Brand Consistency Across Multiple Books

- **Series Branding**
  Use a consistent design for covers in a series so they stand out and look unified on retail pages.
- **Thematic Continuity**
  Maintain elements—like recurring characters, settings, or topics—that encourage readers to move from book to book.
- **Cross-Promotion**
  Link your books together with "Also by this author" pages, ensuring readers know you have more to offer.

Outsourcing Tasks (Editing, Marketing, Design) to Grow Efficiently

- **Hiring Professionals**
  Once you have a steady revenue stream, invest in a professional editor, cover designer, or marketer to take your books to the next level.
- **Virtual Assistants**
  Delegate administrative tasks like scheduling social media posts, managing review requests, or updating metadata so you can focus on writing.
- **Balancing Quality & Cost**
  Develop a budget and hiring plan that prioritizes tasks you can't do well yourself. High-quality work boosts your brand, but be mindful of ROI.

Chapter 19: Legal and Administrative Considerations

As you expand your POD business, you'll need to address the **legal and administrative** aspects that come with being an author-entrepreneur. Safeguarding your intellectual property and staying compliant with local regulations can save headaches down the road.

Copyright Basics and ISBN Requirements

- **Copyright Law**
  In most countries, your written work is automatically protected under copyright law once you create it. However, you may want to register for official copyright, which can provide additional legal benefits in case of infringement.
- **ISBN (International Standard Book Number)**
  An ISBN identifies your book's edition and format. Certain platforms (like Amazon KDP) offer free ISBNs, but using your own can sometimes offer more publishing flexibility.

Tax Obligations and Best Practices

- **Sales Tax & VAT**
  Depending on where you live and where you sell, you may be required to collect and remit sales tax or VAT. Check your local regulations or consult an accountant for clarity.
- **Author Earnings & Income Tax**
  Keep track of royalties from each platform, and stay organized with clear record-keeping. You may need to file quarterly taxes or end-of-year declarations.
- **Business Registration**
  As your income grows, you might consider forming a legal entity (e.g., LLC in the U.S.) for liability protection and potential tax advantages.

Intellectual Property and Plagiarism Concerns

- **Protecting Your Work**
  Regularly search for pirated copies of your book online. If you find unauthorized distributions, issue a DMCA takedown notice.
- **Avoiding Infringement**
  When using quotes, images, or references to real-life products or trademarks, ensure you have the right permissions or that your usage meets fair-use criteria.
- **Plagiarism Checks**
  Keep your content original. Use plagiarism-check software if you collaborate with ghostwriters or outsource portions of your work.

Protecting Yourself and Your Work

- **Contracts & Agreements**
  If you hire an illustrator, editor, or marketer, have clear written agreements detailing ownership of creative assets and deadlines.
- **Disclaimers**
  Include necessary disclaimers (e.g., "This book is for informational purposes only" or "Results may vary") especially if you're writing about health, finance, or legal topics.
- **Professional Advice**
  If you're unsure about legal matters, consult a qualified attorney or publishing professional.

Chapter 20: The Future of Your Print on Demand Journey

By now, you've learned how to write, publish, market, and potentially expand your catalog of POD books. **The journey doesn't stop here**—in fact, this is just the beginning.

Maintaining Momentum and Continuous Improvement

- **Regular Publishing Schedule**
  Consistency keeps readers engaged. Plan your next projects, whether that's new book ideas or updated editions of existing titles.
- **Monitoring Trends**
  Stay aware of industry developments, changing reader preferences, and evolving marketing tactics to remain competitive.
- **Gathering Ongoing Feedback**
  Always be open to reader input. Host Q&A sessions, run polls, or invite beta readers to weigh in on works-in-progress.

Exploring New Book Formats (Audiobooks, Special Editions)

- **Audiobooks**
  Audiobooks are gaining popularity. Consider narrating your work if you have the voice and equipment, or hire a professional narrator through platforms like ACX.
- **Hardcover & Special Editions**
  Offering collector's editions, signed copies, or hardcover versions can attract dedicated fans and generate higher profit margins.
- **Bundles & Box Sets**
  If you have multiple titles, bundling them into a box set can

increase perceived value and encourage readers to buy more of your work at once.

Keeping Up with Industry Changes and Updates

- **Platform Policies**
  Amazon, IngramSpark, Lulu, and others frequently update royalty rates, advertisement options, and content guidelines. Keep an eye on announcements to adapt accordingly.
- **New Marketing Channels**
  Emerging social media platforms or advertising tools can offer untapped audiences. Experiment selectively to find what resonates with your readers.
- **Shifts in Reader Behavior**
  Monitor how consumer habits change—from reading on mobile devices to preferring certain genres at different times of the year.

Final Words of Encouragement and Next Steps

- **Celebrate Milestones**
  Every new book launch, sales milestone, or positive review is cause for celebration. Recognize your achievements to stay motivated.
- **Embrace the Learning Curve**
  The POD landscape evolves constantly. Expect to learn new marketing tactics, adapt to policy changes, and refine your publishing skills continuously.
- **Stay True to Your Vision**
  Ultimately, your passion for writing and connection with readers will drive long-term success. Keep telling the stories or sharing the knowledge you're uniquely suited to provide.

Chapter 21: Maximizing Traffic to Your Etsy Shop – 20 Proven Methods

If you're looking to stand out in a crowded marketplace, driving consistent and quality traffic to your Etsy shop is essential. Below are **20 proven methods** that can help you attract new visitors and convert them into loyal customers.

1. **Leveraging SEO with Fresh Keywords**
   - Conduct regular keyword research (using tools like Etsy's own search bar, eRank, or Marmalead) to keep your listings relevant.
   - Update your titles, tags, and descriptions to match changing search trends.
2. **Optimizing Product Photography and Listing Images**
   - Use bright, clear, and well-lit images.
   - Show multiple angles and context shots (e.g., a T-shirt worn by a model, a mug in a cozy kitchen setting).
3. **Utilizing Pinterest Boards and Group Boards**
   - Pin your product photos to relevant boards.
   - Join group boards in your niche to expand your reach.
4. **Collaborating with Influencers on Instagram or TikTok**
   - Gift influencers or offer them an affiliate arrangement to share your products with their audiences.
   - Look for influencers who align with your brand style and target customer demographics.
5. **Running Targeted Etsy Ads**
   - Use Etsy's internal advertising platform to appear at the top of relevant search results.

- Monitor daily budgets and keywords to refine your strategy over time.

6. **Offering Exclusive Sales and Coupon Codes**
    - Entice first-time buyers with a discount, or reward repeat customers to foster loyalty.
    - Announce limited-time promos on social media to create urgency.

7. **Using Your Blog or Website for Backlinks**
    - Write blog posts featuring your products, linking back to your Etsy listings.
    - Quality backlinks can improve your Etsy shop's overall visibility in search engines.

8. **Guest Posting on Niche Blogs for Visibility**
    - Reach out to popular blogs relevant to your product niche.
    - Provide valuable content and link to your shop for added exposure.

9. **Utilizing Local Markets and Craft Fairs to Drive Online Traffic**
    - Collect email addresses from attendees and hand out business cards with your Etsy URL.
    - Showcasing your products in person can help build brand recognition and trust.

10. **Building an Email List with Freebies or Exclusive Content**

- Offer a discount code or printable guide in exchange for sign-ups.
- Send out regular newsletters with new product announcements and promotions.

11. **Hosting Giveaways and Social Media Contests**

- Encourage participants to follow, share, or tag friends to increase engagement.
- Offer one of your products as the prize to generate excitement around your brand.

12. **Listing New Products Regularly for Algorithm Boosts**

- Etsy's algorithm favors active shops. Introducing fresh items or renewing older listings can keep your shop relevant.
- Frequent updates also give returning customers something new to see.

13. **Encouraging User-Generated Content and Hashtag Campaigns**
- Ask satisfied customers to share photos of your products in action, tagging your brand.
- Repost their images (with permission) to build social proof.

14. **Cross-Promoting on YouTube or Podcast Platforms**
- Create product demos or behind-the-scenes videos to post on YouTube.
- Appear as a guest on podcasts related to your niche to tap into new audiences.

15. **Networking in Facebook Groups Dedicated to Your Niche**
- Offer helpful advice or share your expertise (avoid spamming).
- When relevant, subtly mention or link to your Etsy shop.

16. **Partnering with Other Etsy Sellers for Joint Promotions**
- Offer bundle deals with complementary products.
- Cross-share each other's shops on social media and newsletters.

17. **Featuring Behind-the-Scenes Content to Spark Curiosity**
- Show the design or production process.
- Add a personal touch, helping customers feel connected to your brand story.

18. **Creating a Loyalty or Referral Program**
- Reward repeat buyers with discounts or free shipping after multiple purchases.
- Provide referral bonuses for customers who bring in new buyers.

19. **Incorporating QR Codes in Print Materials**

- Print flyers or stickers featuring a QR code that leads directly to your Etsy shop.
- Perfect for local events, fairs, or even packaging inserts.

20. **Leveraging Seasonal and Holiday Trends**
- Create holiday-themed products or limited-edition collections.
- Utilize relevant seasonal keywords (e.g., "Mother's Day gift," "Halloween décor") to capture timely searches.

Chapter 22: Social Media Marketing for Your POD Brand

Social media can be a powerful marketing tool, especially when you're aiming to stand out in the competitive print-on-demand space. By tailoring your approach to the right platforms and posting compelling content, you'll nurture a community of loyal fans who are more likely to become repeat customers.

Choosing the Right Platforms

- **Audience Analysis**
  Research where your target audience spends the most time. If you're selling quirky apparel, TikTok or Instagram might be ideal; if you cater to business professionals, LinkedIn or Facebook could be more effective.
- **Platform Strengths**
    - Instagram: Visual storytelling, reels, product showcases.
    - TikTok: Short, engaging videos with viral potential.
    - Facebook: Groups and community building.
    - Pinterest: Ideal for evergreen content and product discovery.

Crafting Engaging Content

- **Product Showcases**
  Feature your products in action, highlighting design details or unique selling points.
- **Design Previews & Behind-the-Scenes**
  Give followers a glimpse into your creative process. Let them feel invested in your brand by witnessing new designs before they launch.
- **Interactive Elements**
  Use polls, Q&A sessions, or quizzes to encourage direct engagement.

Scheduling & Consistency

- **Content Calendar**
  Plan out your posts for at least a month in advance. This helps maintain a steady flow of updates without overwhelming you.
- **Batch Work**
  Create multiple social media posts in one sitting. This saves time and ensures cohesive branding.
- **Management Tools**
  Platforms like Hootsuite, Buffer, or Later let you schedule posts and analyze performance in one place.

Analytics & Adjustments

- **Track Engagement Metrics**
  Pay close attention to likes, shares, saves, and comments—these indicators show how well your content resonates with your audience.
- **Refine Your Strategy**
  If certain posts perform well, repeat or expand on similar themes. If others flop, analyze why and adapt accordingly.
- **Set Goals**
  Aim to grow your following, boost click-through rates to

your shop, and ultimately increase sales. Adjust your content plan as you learn what works best.

Chapter 23: Collaboration & Partnerships

Collaborations can be a game-changer for print-on-demand entrepreneurs. By partnering with other creators, brands, or influencers, you broaden your reach and build trust through third-party endorsements.

Working with Fellow Creators

- **Co-Launch Collections**
  Join forces with another artist, designer, or craftsperson to create a collaborative product line. This introduces each of you to a fresh audience.
- **Joint Giveaways**
  Pool resources to offer bigger, more enticing prizes. Share the giveaway across both audiences for maximum exposure.
- **Cross-Promoting Designs**
  Feature each other's products in your respective shops or social media channels.

Brand Partnerships

- **Complementary Products**
  Align with companies that offer products which naturally pair with yours (e.g., a mug maker teaming up with a tea brand, or a tote bag designer collaborating with a book subscription service).
- **Shared Audiences**
  Look for businesses with a similar aesthetic or customer base but non-competing product lines. You'll each benefit from the mutual cross-promotion.
- **Bundled Offerings**
  Create special bundle deals—one item from each business—that shoppers can purchase at a discount.

Affiliate and Influencer Marketing

- **Setting Up an Affiliate Program**
  Use affiliate software (or Etsy's own affiliate program if available) to track sales and pay commissions. This motivates content creators to promote your brand.
- **Influencer Outreach**
  Identify influencers who align with your brand ethos and style. Offer them sample products or a unique discount code for their followers.
- **Measuring Results**
  Track which affiliates or influencer campaigns generate the most sales. Focus on building long-term relationships with high performers.

Chapter 24: Expanding to Amazon – KDP and Merch by Amazon

Many creators begin their print-on-demand journey on Etsy, but once you've established a solid foundation, it can be beneficial to branch out to the world's largest online marketplace—**Amazon**. From self-publishing books to selling custom T-shirts, you'll find multiple avenues to reach Amazon's massive global audience.

Deciding Your Approach

- **KDP (Kindle Direct Publishing) for Books**
  Ideal if you're writing or producing books, such as novels, children's books, or nonfiction guides. KDP offers both paperback and Kindle eBook formats.
- **Merch by Amazon for Apparel and More**
  Geared toward T-shirts, hoodies, pop sockets, and other branded merchandise. You upload designs, choose products, and Amazon handles printing and shipping.

Each program targets different product types and has distinct royalty structures. Consider your current expertise and what resonates with your audience before deciding which path—or if both—suits your business best.

Listing & Optimization

- **Apply Etsy SEO Lessons**
  Just as you researched keywords for Etsy, identify relevant Amazon keywords using tools like Amazon's own search autocomplete, Publisher Rocket, or other keyword analyzers.
- **High-Impact Titles & Descriptions**
  Write clear, concise product descriptions, highlighting unique benefits. Incorporate your best keywords naturally.

- **Quality Covers & Images**
  For KDP books, a compelling cover greatly influences conversions. For Merch, ensure your design thumbnail is eye-catching and reflective of your brand.

Prime Benefits & Global Reach

- **Prime Shipping**
  Amazon Prime members often prefer products with free, fast shipping. If your print-on-demand items qualify, you may see a boost in conversions.
- **International Markets**
  Amazon has separate marketplaces in various countries (e.g., .com, .co.uk, .de). Consider enabling international shipping or listing directly in those regions to expand your customer base.

Challenges & Fees

- **Competition**
  Amazon is a crowded marketplace. Regularly monitor your niche to stay ahead of emerging trends and designs.
- **Platform Fees**
  While KDP allows free uploading, Merch by Amazon is invite-only (though you can request an invitation). Both have specific royalty and payout structures you'll need to review.
- **Policy Compliance**
  Amazon policies can be strict. Stay up to date with content guidelines, royalty rules, and intellectual property restrictions to avoid penalties.

Chapter 25: Harnessing the Power of Shopify

If you're looking for **total control** over your storefront—from design to customer interactions—**Shopify** might be the next logical step. By building a standalone store, you can cultivate your brand identity, set up custom features, and keep more profit by avoiding marketplace fees.

Why Shopify?

- **Branding Freedom**
  Unlike Etsy or Amazon, there are fewer design limitations. Customize your site layout, color schemes, and overall user experience.
- **Ownership of Customer Data**
  You collect emails and manage your customer relationships directly, making it easier to build a loyal following and remarket to them.
- **No Marketplace Fees**
  While Shopify has a monthly subscription fee, you won't lose a percentage of each sale to a marketplace platform—beyond standard payment processing.

Choosing POD Integrations

- **Printify, Printful, and More**
  These services integrate seamlessly with Shopify, automating order fulfillment. Once a customer buys from your Shopify store, the chosen POD provider prints and ships directly to them.
- **Evaluating Quality & Costs**
  Compare providers for their print quality, shipping times, and base costs. Some may offer specific product lines that fit your brand better.

Building a Professional Storefront

- **Picking Themes**
  Shopify offers free and premium themes. Choose one that matches your brand's aesthetic and offers the functionality you need (e.g., product sliders, featured collections).
- **Customizing Pages**
  Add an "About Us" page, FAQs, and clear policies. Streamline your navigation so customers can easily find product categories.
- **Seamless Checkout Experience**
  Ensure your checkout is clean and straightforward. Minimize distractions or extra steps that could lead to cart abandonment.

Marketing & Apps

- **Shopify App Store**
  Access tools for SEO, email marketing, retargeting ads, upselling, and more. Many apps offer free plans or trials, so test a few to see which best suits your shop.
- **Email Marketing Integration**
  Services like Klaviyo, Mailchimp, or Omnisend allow you to set up automated email flows, such as welcome sequences or abandoned cart reminders.
- **Social Media Sync**
  Easily connect Shopify to your social channels, enabling features like Instagram product tagging or Facebook Shop integration.

Chapter 26: Building a Multi-Channel Brand

Selling on multiple platforms—Etsy, Amazon, Shopify, and even others—can drive more revenue and brand awareness. However, you'll need a strategic plan to keep everything cohesive and well-organized.

Developing a Consistent Brand Identity

- **Uniform Aesthetics**
  Use the same logos, color schemes, and fonts across all platforms, from your Etsy shop banner to your Shopify homepage.
- **Consistent Messaging**
  Whether you're writing an Amazon product description or an Instagram caption, maintain a unified brand voice.

Inventory & Listing Management

- **Syncing Product Data**
  Tools like Sellbrite or Shopify's channel integrations can help you list and update products across platforms from one dashboard.
- **Avoiding Stock-Outs**
  Ensure your POD providers have accurate inventory details. If you introduce limited-edition designs, monitor sales closely to prevent overselling.

Pricing Strategies

- **Coherent Pricing Across Platforms**
  While fees differ among Etsy, Amazon, and Shopify, keep your retail prices consistent when possible to avoid confusing customers.
- **Factoring in Fees**
  Carefully calculate total costs (transaction fees, platform subscriptions, shipping) to ensure you maintain healthy profit margins.

Customer Experience

- **Unified Communication**
  Provide similar response times and customer service quality whether someone messages you on Etsy or via Shopify's chat widget.
- **Packaging & Branding**
  Even though POD items ship directly from providers, you can often include custom branding elements like stickers or inserts.
- **Post-Purchase Support**
  Follow up with buyers for feedback and offer easy returns, regardless of which platform they used to purchase.

Chapter 27: Cross-Selling, Upselling, and Bundling

When you're operating in a competitive space, you need to make the most of each customer visit. **Cross-selling, upselling, and bundling** are powerful tactics for increasing your average order value (AOV) and delighting customers with complementary products.

Product Bundles

- **Combining Complementary Items**
  Pair a matching T-shirt and mug set, or design-themed bundles for events like weddings or baby showers.
- **Themed Bundles**
  Example: A "Coffee Lover Bundle" could include a coffee-themed mug, T-shirt, and tote bag—all at a slightly discounted rate.

Upselling Techniques

- **Limited-Edition Variants**
  Offer a higher-priced version of a product with exclusive design elements or premium materials.
- **Checkout Suggestions**
  Display an upgraded item or related design at checkout to capture last-minute impulse purchases.

Customer Journey Maps

- **Understanding User Flow**
  Analyze how shoppers navigate your store, from landing pages to cart checkout. Identify drop-off points to optimize product recommendations.
- **Recommended Products**
  Strategically place "You May Also Like" or "Frequently

Bought Together" sections to encourage additional purchases.

Bundling for Different Seasons

- **Seasonal Gift Sets**
  Create festive bundles for holidays like Christmas, Halloween, or Mother's Day to cater to gift-buying shoppers.
- **Limited-Time Offers**
  Tap into urgency by letting buyers know a holiday bundle is only available for a short period, driving more immediate conversions.

Chapter 28: Streamlining Fulfillment and Logistics

As your print-on-demand (POD) business grows, managing **fulfillment and logistics** efficiently becomes paramount. Whether you're selling on Etsy, Shopify, or multiple marketplaces, a well-structured approach to shipping, quality control, and customer support will help you keep buyers happy—and coming back.

Multi-Warehouse Solutions

- **Localized Print Providers**
  If you sell internationally, consider using multiple POD providers or fulfillment centers. This reduces shipping costs and delivery times for overseas customers.
- **Seamless Integration**
  Platforms like Printify or Printful often let you choose which print facility handles each order based on the buyer's location, minimizing transit time and potential customs delays.
- **Evaluating Partners**
  Look at each provider's production speed, print quality, and overall reliability before deciding to distribute your manufacturing across regions.

Automated Shipping & Tracking

- **Syncing Orders**
  Integrate shipping solutions (e.g., ShipStation, ShipBob) or use the built-in tools from your e-commerce platform. Automated tracking updates keep customers informed.
- **Real-Time Notifications**
  Let buyers receive notifications via email or text as soon as orders ship. This helps reduce customer inquiries about delivery status.

- **Multiple Shipping Options**
  Offer various shipping tiers (standard, expedited, international) to cater to different customer needs and budgets.

Quality Control

- **Sample Orders**
  Periodically order samples from your chosen POD providers to check print quality, color accuracy, and packaging.
- **Packaging Verification**
  If possible, specify packaging materials or include branded inserts, so your products arrive in excellent condition—and with a memorable unboxing experience.
- **Reducing Returns**
  Detailed product descriptions, sizing charts, and high-quality images minimize customer dissatisfaction. Clear return policies also set realistic expectations.

Scaling Customer Service

- **Hiring Virtual Assistants**
  Once you're receiving multiple orders per day, it might be time to hire help. Virtual assistants can manage email inquiries, handle refunds, and follow up on order statuses.
- **Response Time Goals**
  Aim to reply to customer messages within 24 hours (or sooner if possible). Quick, friendly communication increases buyer satisfaction.
- **Automated FAQs**
  Use chatbots or a well-organized FAQ section to handle common questions about shipping, returns, or product details.

Chapter 29: Data-Driven Growth & Automation

To keep your POD enterprise thriving, you'll need to **measure performance** and make informed decisions. Embracing **analytics tools** and automation can save you time, reduce errors, and optimize the customer journey.

Analytics Tools

- **Platform Dashboards**
  Shopify, Etsy, and Amazon each provide native analytics on traffic sources, conversion rates, and sales figures.
- **Google Analytics**
  Track where your visitors come from, how they navigate your site, and which pages lead to the most conversions.
- **Conversion Funnels**
  Identify high-exit pages or steps in the checkout process where customers abandon their carts.

Sales Funnel Optimization

- **Mapping the Customer Journey**
  From initial site visit or product view to checkout, understand how customers move through each stage.
- **Retargeting Ads**
  Use platforms like Facebook Ads or Google Ads to bring back visitors who left without purchasing.
- **Abandoned Cart Emails**
  Remind hesitant buyers to complete their purchase by offering a small discount or free shipping if they return.

Setting Up Automation

- **Tools & Platforms**
  Automation tools like Zapier, IFTTT, or Integromat

connect different apps and services to handle repetitive tasks.
- **Streamlined Marketing**
  Automate email campaigns for new subscribers, loyalty rewards, and follow-up thank-you messages post-purchase.
- **Social Media Scheduling**
  Batch your social media content and schedule it via tools like Buffer, Hootsuite, or Later so you can focus on higher-level tasks.

Continuous Improvement

- **A/B Testing**
  Test variations of product titles, images, descriptions, or pricing to see which performs best.
- **Iterative Design Updates**
  If a certain style or layout yields a better response, apply that format across your listings or pages.
- **Customer Feedback Loops**
  Encourage reviews and surveys to gather insights on what you can improve next. Over time, these incremental tweaks can substantially boost your conversion rates.

Chapter 30: Future Innovations and Trends in POD

The print-on-demand sector is constantly evolving. Staying attuned to **emerging trends and technologies** will help you keep your business relevant and open new opportunities for growth.

Sustainability and Eco-Friendly Products

- **Eco-Conscious Materials**
  More consumers prioritize ethical and sustainable products. Research POD partners that use organic fabrics, recycled packaging, or water-based inks.
- **Transparent Practices**
  Highlight your commitment to eco-friendly options. Customers appreciate brands with clear sustainability goals.
- **Long-Term Impact**
  Adopting green practices can also reduce waste and potentially lower costs in the long run.

Emerging Marketing Channels

- **New Social Platforms**
  Keep an eye on emerging apps (e.g., Clubhouse, newer TikTok alternatives) where early adopters can gain significant traction.
- **Voice Search & AI**
  As voice-activated devices grow in popularity, optimize your product listings for verbal commands and explore AI-driven personalization.
- **Virtual & Augmented Reality**
  Innovative brands may experiment with AR tools that let buyers "try" products virtually before purchasing.

Interactive & Personalized Products

- **Customization Options**
  Many POD providers now allow on-demand personalization—let customers add names, dates, or unique messages to designs.
- **Build-a-Product Experiences**
  Offering a step-by-step "design your own" feature can drastically boost engagement and satisfaction.
- **Community Involvement**
  Use polls or surveys so customers can vote on new design ideas, making them feel invested in your brand.

Long-Term Vision

- **Continual Growth**
  As your product catalog expands, consider rolling out new collections or premium lines.
- **Experimentation**
  Test new niches or product lines to diversify your income. What starts as a small experiment could become a major profit center.
- **Adaptability**
  Industry changes, consumer preferences, and new technologies can shift quickly. Remaining agile and open to new ideas is key to sustaining success.

Chapter 31: Embracing the Journey from Day One

Starting your print-on-demand (POD) adventure is both thrilling and intimidating. From choosing your niche to uploading your first design, you might initially feel a surge of excitement—quickly followed by uncertainty. This chapter is all about **harnessing that initial enthusiasm** and using it as fuel for the road ahead.

A Fresh Beginning

- **Mindset over Mechanics**
  Your attitude and determination matter as much—if not more—than technical know-how. While it's important to learn best practices, it's even more crucial to believe in your ability to grow and adapt.
- **Setting Realistic Expectations**
  Everyone's timeline looks different. Comparing your Day One to someone else's Year Three sets you up for discouragement. Recognize that each seller's journey is unique, and focus on steady personal progress rather than quick success.

Tips for Positive Beginnings

1. **Celebrate Small Steps**
   Successfully formatting your first product listing is a win, even if you haven't sold a single item yet. Acknowledge each accomplishment to build confidence and momentum.
2. **Build Early Support**
   Share your plans with friends, family, or an online community. Their encouragement can sustain you through tough spots—plus, they may become your first customers or give valuable feedback.
3. **Journal Your Process**
   Keeping a record of what you learn each day or week

provides perspective later when you see how far you've come. Revisiting past entries helps you appreciate your progress and identify areas for improvement.

Chapter 32: Pushing Through the Dip – Surviving the "No Results" Phase

Almost every POD seller hits a point where sales are slow and doubts creep in. This "dip" can feel like an endless rut, making you question whether the effort is worth it. However, it's often the period **just before significant growth**—if you persist.

Recognizing the Dip

- **What It Looks Like**
  You've launched multiple products, but you're not seeing consistent orders or the traction you hoped for. Website traffic might be minimal, and engagement on your listings could feel stagnant.
- **Why It Happens**
  Building brand awareness, refining SEO, and honing in on a target audience can all take time. Success rarely comes overnight; often it's about incremental improvements.

Strategies for Overcoming the Slow Period

1. **Revisit Your Analytics**
   Data doesn't lie. Examine which products get the most views, clicks, or favorites, then double down on what's working. If a certain design or listing converts better, try creating more variations or similar styles.

2. **Optimize Overhaul**
   Refresh your listings—update keywords, rewrite descriptions, or add new, high-quality images. Minor tweaks can significantly impact your visibility in search results.
3. **Stay Visible**
   Maintain a social media presence, blog updates, or email newsletters. Consistency fosters trust and keeps your products top-of-mind for potential buyers.

The Upside of the Dip

- **Building Resilience**
  Surviving these slow phases teaches you adaptability—a crucial trait for long-term success in any business.
- **Learning and Iterating**
  Each challenge is a chance to refine your approach, making future endeavors more effective. The lessons you learn now can accelerate your growth later.

Chapter 33: Reflecting on Your Why – Connecting with Your Core Purpose

When self-doubt looms large, **remembering your "why"** can ground you and keep you moving forward. Whether it's a passion for art, a drive to supplement your income, or a dream of building a global brand—keep that motivation front and center.

The Power of Purpose

- **Guiding Principle**
  Your "why" can guide every decision you make, from which products you create to the way you interact with customers. A clear purpose also fosters consistency in your brand message.
- **Emotional Anchoring**
  On days when you feel like quitting, recalling your deeper reason for starting can reignite your determination. This emotional spark often carries you through tough moments.

Exercises to Clarify Your Why

1. **Visualize Success**
   Picture what your life looks like once your POD business thrives. Who benefits from your success? How do you feel each morning when you start working?
2. **Create a Vision Board**
   Collage images, quotes, and words that represent your goals—place it where you'll see it daily. Constant visual reminders keep you aligned with your aspirations.
3. **Journal Prompts**
   Write about what drew you to POD initially and how achieving success would change your life. Revisiting these

entries strengthens your sense of purpose when doubt arises.

Chapter 34: Mastering Self-Motivation – Overcoming the Urge to Quit

As an entrepreneur, you won't always have a boss or teammates pushing you. **Cultivating self-motivation** ensures that, even when external results lag, you have an internal drive to keep going.

Common Obstacles to Motivation

- **Fear of Failure**
  Worrying about potential losses or embarrassment can paralyze you from taking action. Recognize that every success story includes missteps and failures along the way.
- **Perfectionism**
  Insisting on flawless designs or descriptions can slow your progress—sometimes done is better than perfect. Over time, you'll refine and improve.

Tactics to Boost Internal Drive

1. **Micro-Goals**
   Break tasks into bite-sized pieces. Completing small objectives regularly builds momentum and keeps you motivated.
2. **Positive Self-Talk**
   How you speak to yourself can shape your motivation. Replace "I can't do this" with "I'm still learning" or "I'll find a way."
3. **Accountability Buddies**
   Share daily or weekly goals with a fellow entrepreneur or friend. Having mutual check-ins can be a powerful motivator.

Converting Setbacks into Fuel

- **Reframe Failures**
  Each failed design or low sales month holds lessons for future decisions. Instead of dwelling on what went wrong, focus on how you'll adapt.
- **Iterate Quickly**
  The faster you learn from a misstep and adjust your approach, the closer you get to a breakthrough. Embrace continuous improvement as part of the process.

Chapter 35: Celebrating Milestones – Turning Small Wins into Big Momentum

When you're deeply focused on lofty end goals, it's easy to forget to celebrate the small victories along the way. However, **acknowledging each milestone—no matter how minor—can boost morale and spark continued progress.** Think of these small wins as building blocks that pave the path to greater success.

Why Small Wins Matter

- **Validation & Confidence**
  Each win reassures you that you're on the right path, fueling even bigger aspirations. Milestones act as checkpoints, confirming that your time and energy are paying off.
- **Motivation Amplifier**
  Recognizing progress creates excitement and a renewed drive to tackle new challenges. When you acknowledge a minor achievement, you remind yourself you're capable of reaching bigger goals, too.

Ways to Celebrate

1. **Public Announcements**
   Post on social media when you sell your 10th item, or when you introduce a new product line. Share your excitement—your audience will likely celebrate with you.
2. **Personal Rewards**
   Treat yourself to something enjoyable—like a favorite meal, a small gift, or a relaxing afternoon off—when you hit a goal. These rewards can boost morale and energize you for the next phase.

3. **Gratitude Practice**
   At the end of each week, note what went well—be it a nice review or a small sales bump. Focusing on positives helps you see growth rather than setbacks.

Sustaining the Energy

- **Milestone Roadmap**
  Lay out specific markers (e.g., 100 sales, 1,000 social media followers) and plan small celebratory actions in advance. This not only gives you something to look forward to but also helps maintain momentum.
- **Share the Joy**
  Involve supporters—customers, friends, and family—in your celebration. Their excitement enhances your own, and they'll feel more invested in your journey.

Chapter 36: Deepening Your Creative Process – Tapping Into New Sources of Inspiration

A thriving print-on-demand (POD) enterprise relies on **fresh, standout designs, engaging product ideas, and authenticity**. If you find your creativity stagnating, it's time to explore new inspiration and try innovative techniques that can reinvigorate both you and your brand.

Exploring Fresh Inspiration

- **Travel & Culture**
  Immerse yourself in local art shows, music events, or even virtual tours of world museums. Stepping out of your everyday routine often sparks fresh concepts.
- **Nature & Outdoors**
  Taking walks, hiking, or simply sitting in a park can clear mental clutter and open you to new ideas. Sometimes, the best inspirations come when you're unplugged from technology.
- **Online Inspiration**
  Browsing Pinterest, Behance, or Dribbble can stimulate new approaches—but be mindful not to copy others' work. Instead, use what you see as a springboard for your own creativity.

Experimenting with New Techniques

- **Mixed Media**
  Combine different styles—hand-drawn elements, digital effects, or photography—to create designs that stand out. Blending mediums can lead to distinctive, eye-catching products.

- **Creative Constraints**
  Challenge yourself: design a product using only two colors or focus on a single theme for a week. Constraints force you to think differently, often leading to unexpectedly innovative results.

Sustaining Creative Growth

1. **Regular Brainstorm Sessions**
   Schedule weekly or monthly idea dumps where you jot down every design concept, no matter how wild. Reviewing these ideas later can spark new directions for your shop.
2. **Artistic Collaborations**
   Team up with other creators—an illustrator, a photographer, a writer—to expand your repertoire. Collaborative projects can infuse fresh perspectives into your designs.
3. **Ongoing Skill Development**
   Take online classes in illustration, typography, or branding. The more skills you have, the more varied and compelling your designs become.

A Few Thoughts on Motivation and Creativity

Launching and running a POD business can be an **emotional rollercoaster**. You'll experience moments of exhilarating progress—and times of stagnant sales or wavering self-belief. By **finding your why**, **mastering self-motivation**, and **welcoming creative exploration**, you'll cultivate the resilience you need to keep going.

Remember: each hurdle is an invitation to **innovate, learn, and grow**. With persistent effort and an open heart, you'll gradually transform your vision into a thriving reality. Your journey is a testament to your dedication, and every step—big or small—brings you closer to the success you've envisioned.

Chapter 37: Mastering the Art of Design Trends

Content Overview:
As the print-on-demand market grows more competitive, staying on top of design trends can help your products stand out. This chapter explores how to predict, analyze, and implement emerging styles, ensuring that your POD catalog remains fresh and appealing to modern consumers.

Subsections

1. **Analyzing Seasonal and Yearly Design Trends**
    - **Trend Cycles:** Understanding how styles rise and fall over time, including annual holiday surges and seasonal shifts (e.g., winter motifs, summer color palettes).
    - **Translating Trends into Products:** Adapting what's "in" to your niche (e.g., minimalist T-shirts, playful mug designs) while maintaining your brand identity.
2. **Incorporating Cultural and Regional Preferences**
    - **Geographic Trends:** Why certain colors, symbols, or themes resonate in specific countries or regions.
    - **Cultural Sensitivity:** How to respectfully incorporate cultural elements without veering into appropriation or stereotypes.
3. **Tools for Trend Forecasting**

- **Pinterest & Instagram:** Spotting viral aesthetics, hashtags, and mood boards that gain traction.
- **Google Trends & Keyword Tools:** Tracking rising search terms to anticipate shifts in buyer interest.
- **Influencer & Brand Collaborations:** Keeping an eye on what major influencers and brands are promoting to glean upcoming trends.

Chapter 38: Customer Persona Development

Content Overview:
A well-defined customer persona helps streamline your marketing, product designs, and overall brand strategy. This chapter explains how to identify and understand your ideal customer, enabling you to create products that genuinely resonate.

Subsections

1. **Creating Detailed Customer Personas**
    - **Demographics & Psychographics:** Pinpointing age range, occupation, lifestyle preferences, values, and buying habits.
    - **Personal Goals & Pain Points:** Determining what your customer hopes to achieve or solve with your products (e.g., self-expression, gift-giving needs).
2. **Aligning Product Designs with Customer Preferences**
    - **Theme & Style Consistency:** Ensuring that your product lines appeal to the persona's tastes (e.g., colorful designs for a youthful audience, minimalist for a more professional crowd).
    - **Customer Feedback Loops:** Using reviews, polls, or social media comments to refine products and confirm that designs hit the mark.
3. **Using Analytics to Refine Your Audience**
    - **Etsy, Shopify, and Google Analytics:** Identifying where traffic comes from, what keywords drive clicks, and which listings convert best.
    - **Iterative Persona Updates:** Adapting your customer persona as your business grows and you discover new market segments.

Chapter 39: Crafting the Perfect Product Bundle

Content Overview:
Product bundles can increase the average order value (AOV) and offer a convenient shopping experience for customers. This chapter delves into how to strategically create and market bundled items to boost sales and customer satisfaction.

Subsections

1. **Types of Bundles (e.g., Thematic, Functional)**
   - **Thematic Bundles:** Grouping items around a central theme (e.g., a "Cozy Winter" set with a blanket, mug, and candle).
   - **Functional Bundles:** Curating products that serve a practical purpose together (e.g., a matching T-shirt and tote bag for eco-conscious shoppers).
2. **Pricing Strategies for Bundles**
   - **Perceived Value vs. Actual Cost:** Determining discounts that entice buyers without sacrificing margins.
   - **Tiered Bundling:** Offering basic, premium, and deluxe bundles to accommodate varying budgets and preferences.
3. **Tools to Test and Promote Bundles Effectively**
   - **A/B Testing:** Trying different bundle compositions, product images, and price points to find the best performers.
   - **Cross-Channel Promotion:** Showcasing bundles on social media, email newsletters, and within your Etsy or Shopify listings to maximize visibility.

Chapter 40: Evolving with Market Shifts and Innovation

Content Overview:
The print-on-demand landscape is dynamic—consumer preferences, technology, and global trends can change swiftly. This final chapter helps readers anticipate shifts and stay adaptable, ensuring their business remains competitive and future-ready.

Subsections

1. **Monitoring Market and Tech Trends**
   - **Emerging Product Types:** From new wearables to eco-friendly materials that could reshape the POD industry.
   - **AI and Personalization:** How automated design or personalization features can elevate user experience.
2. **Flexible Business Strategies**
   - **Pivoting Quickly:** Recognizing when a certain niche or design style is declining, and how to adapt swiftly.
   - **Diversification:** Expanding product lines, exploring new sales channels, or adding collaborations to spread risk.
3. **Building a Culture of Innovation**
   - **Ongoing Experimentation:** Regularly testing fresh ideas, whether it's new design software or marketing platforms.

- **Community Feedback:** Keeping an open dialogue with customers to co-create products they truly want.

Chapter 40: Building Resilience During Market Slumps

Content Overview:
Even the most successful POD sellers face low sales periods. Instead of viewing these slumps as business failures, this chapter presents them as opportunities to **regroup, diversify, and refine** your business strategy. Readers will discover how to stay motivated and emerge from slow seasons with greater focus and innovation.

Subsections

1. **Diversifying Income Streams**
    - **Beyond Single Platforms:** Listing your products on multiple marketplaces (e.g., Amazon, Shopify) to minimize risk.
    - **Digital Products & Services:** Offering downloadable designs, online courses, or consulting to supplement POD revenue.
2. **Leveraging Slow Periods for Skill Development**
    - **Upskilling & Experimentation:** Using downtime to learn new design tools, try fresh techniques, or explore untapped niches.

        ○ **Brand Refresh:** Evaluating your branding, product photography, and storefront layout to make improvements without the pressure of high-volume orders.
    3. **Seasonal Planning and Preparing for Spikes**
        ○ **Holiday & Event Calendars:** Identifying key shopping seasons (e.g., Mother's Day, back-to-school) and planning inventory or marketing campaigns well in advance.
        ○ **Building a Launch Roadmap:** Creating teaser campaigns, special offers, and timely promotions to capitalize on busy periods.

Chapter 41: Innovative Marketing Beyond the Basics

Content Overview:
While traditional marketing tactics—like Etsy SEO and social media ads—are crucial, standing out in a saturated marketplace often requires **innovative and creative marketing** approaches. This chapter delves into advanced strategies that are particularly suited for POD sellers seeking fresh, impactful ways to connect with potential buyers.

Subsections

1. **Leveraging User-Generated Content (UGC)**
    ○ **UGC Campaigns:** Encouraging customers to share photos or videos featuring your products in real-life scenarios.

- **Authenticity & Trust:** Demonstrating genuine customer satisfaction can convert curious browsers into paying customers.
2. **Collaborations with Micro-Influencers**
     - **Why Micro-Influencers?** They often have more engaged, loyal followings than large-scale influencers—and typically cost less.
     - **Finding the Right Fit:** Matching your brand aesthetic and values with influencers whose audience aligns with your ideal customer persona.
3. **Implementing Augmented Reality for Product Previews**
     - **AR Basics:** How augmented reality apps and filters can let buyers "try on" or visualize products before purchase.
     - **Low-Cost AR Solutions:** Exploring easy-to-use platforms that don't require expensive custom coding.

Chapter 42: The Psychology of Pricing

Content Overview:
Pricing can make or break a sale—especially in a competitive POD environment. This chapter examines **how psychological factors** influence customers' purchase decisions, offering readers strategies to optimize pricing for maximum profitability and appeal.

Subsections

1. **Psychological Pricing Techniques**
   - **Charm Pricing:** Ending prices in .99 or .95 to make them appear more attractive (e.g., $19.99 vs. $20).
   - **Anchor Pricing:** Showcasing a higher "original" price alongside a discounted price to emphasize savings.
2. **Testing Price Points Using A/B Methods**
   - **Incremental Adjustments:** Changing a product's price by small amounts over time, tracking conversions to identify sweet spots.
   - **Platform-Specific Considerations:** How Amazon, Etsy, or Shopify might require slightly different pricing strategies due to fees and competition.
3. **Perceived Value vs. Actual Cost**
   - **Brand Positioning:** Convincing customers that your products justify a certain price through design quality, unique features, or brand story.

- **Balancing Profit & Customer Satisfaction:** Ensuring your prices remain fair while covering production, shipping, and marketplace fees.

Chapter 43: Nurturing a Loyal Community for Long-Term Growth

Content Overview:
In today's online marketplace, **community engagement** can be as powerful as any paid marketing campaign. This chapter explains how to foster authentic relationships with customers and fans to create a thriving ecosystem around your brand.

Subsections

1. **Brand-Building Through Engagement**
   - **Interactive Platforms:** Hosting live Q&A sessions or design polls on Instagram, Facebook, or TikTok.
   - **Exclusive Groups:** Launching private Facebook or Discord communities for fans and repeat buyers.
2. **Encouraging Customer Advocacy**
   - **Referral & Reward Programs:** Motivating existing customers to spread the word by offering discounts or loyalty points.
   - **Spotlighting Community Members:** Featuring happy customers' stories, photos, or product experiences to inspire others.
3. **Long-Term Relationship Strategies**
   - **Consistent Communication:** Sharing behind-the-scenes updates, success milestones, or upcoming product previews keeps buyers invested.
   - **Adapting to Feedback:** Actively incorporating suggestions or critique from your community to

refine offerings, demonstrating you value their input.

Chapter 44: Sustainable Practices in POD

Content Overview:
Eco-friendly approaches are increasingly important in e-commerce. This chapter provides **practical ways** to incorporate sustainability into your print-on-demand business, appealing to a growing segment of conscious consumers while reducing environmental impact.

Subsections

1. **Finding Eco-Friendly Print Providers**
   - **Materials & Inks:** Look for suppliers that use organic cotton, recycled paper, or water-based inks.
   - **Certifications & Standards:** Familiarize yourself with labels like GOTS (Global Organic Textile Standard) or FSC (Forest Stewardship Council).
2. **Marketing Sustainability as a Selling Point**
   - **Storytelling:** Highlight your eco-friendly processes in product descriptions, social media posts, and packaging inserts.
   - **Transparency:** Offer data on reduced waste, carbon footprint, or responsible sourcing. Customers appreciate honesty and clarity.
3. **Case Studies of Successful Green Businesses**
   - **Spotlighting Brands:** Examine real-life examples of POD shops that effectively combined profitability with environmentally friendly practices.
   - **Takeaways for Your Shop:** Identify best practices you can adopt or adapt, from packaging choices to ethical labor considerations.

Chapter 45: Future-Proofing Your Etsy POD Business

Content Overview:
Etsy and the POD industry evolve constantly, influenced by new technologies, shifts in consumer behavior, and marketplace policy changes. This chapter guides you in **anticipating and adapting** to these developments, ensuring your shop remains relevant and resilient.

Subsections

1. **Emerging Technologies (e.g., AI, Blockchain)**
    - **AI in Design & Marketing:** How AI-powered tools can streamline design creation, keyword research, and targeted advertising.
    - **Blockchain & NFTs:** An overview of how digital ownership could impact future product offerings or certificate-of-authenticity concepts.
2. **Adapting to Shifts in Consumer Behavior**
    - **Personalization Trends:** Customers increasingly expect customizable products—learn how to offer easy personalization options without sacrificing efficiency.
    - **Omnichannel Experiences:** Providing seamless shopping and customer service across Etsy, social media, and your own website.
3. **Preparing for Marketplace Policy Updates**
    - **Staying Informed:** Follow Etsy's Seller Handbook, community forums, and official announcements for policy changes.

- **Pivoting Quickly:** Develop contingency plans for new fee structures, algorithm tweaks, or listing requirements.

Chapter 46: Global Expansion and Localization

Content Overview:
Reaching international audiences can significantly boost sales and brand awareness. This chapter delves into **expanding your POD business worldwide**, addressing cultural nuances, shipping complexities, and localized marketing.

Subsections

1. **Identifying Key International Markets**
   - **Market Research:** Pinpoint countries or regions with high demand for your niche. Use tools like Google Trends and Etsy's own analytics to gauge interest.
   - **Economic Factors:** Understand local purchasing power and currency considerations to set competitive yet profitable prices.
2. **Navigating Shipping and Logistics**
   - **Multiple Fulfillment Centers:** Collaborate with POD providers that have facilities in different regions, reducing shipping costs and delivery times.
   - **Customs & Duties:** Be transparent about potential import fees to avoid surprises for international customers.
3. **Adapting Products and Marketing Materials**
   - **Localization Basics:** Translate product titles, descriptions, and promotional content for international audiences.

- **Cultural Sensitivity:** Tailor designs and marketing campaigns to local references, festivals, and holidays.

Next Steps and Implementation

You've now explored the process of creating, publishing, and marketing a book through print on demand. To turn these insights into a tangible product, it's important to plan strategically and break everything down into actionable steps. Below is a concise roadmap to guide you from concept to launch.

1. Finalize Your Topic

- **Clarify Your Focus**
  Decide whether you're writing a children's book, a nonfiction guide, a novel, or a specialized how-to. Hone in on a subject you're passionate about or well-versed in—this will help you stay motivated and produce a higher-quality book.
- **Validate Your Idea**
  Conduct market research to confirm there's an audience for your topic. Look at best-seller lists, relevant keywords, and competing titles to gauge potential interest.

2. Create a Writing Schedule

- **Break Down Chapters**
  Outline the tasks for each chapter—research, drafting, editing—and assign an estimated timeframe to each.
- **Set Realistic Deadlines**
  Factor in your personal schedule and responsibilities. Be generous with time estimates to avoid burnout and ensure the final product meets your quality standards.
- **Use Productivity Tools**
  Consider software like Trello, Asana, or Google Calendar to track milestones and stay organized.

---

3. Budget and Resources

- **Determine Your Budget**
  Decide how much you're willing (or able) to spend. Expenses may include editing, cover design, formatting, and marketing.
- **Decide Where to DIY vs. Outsource**
  - **DIY**: Writing, basic formatting, or creating a draft cover in Canva.
  - **Outsource**: Professional editing, cover design, specialized marketing services.
- **Allocate Funds Wisely**
  If you can only afford one big expense, consider hiring an experienced editor or cover designer—both are crucial to attracting and retaining readers.

---

4. Gather Tools and Accounts

- **Choose a POD Platform**
  Options include Amazon KDP, IngramSpark, Lulu, and more. Each has different features, fees, and distribution channels.

- **Sign Up & Review Guidelines**
  Create an account on your chosen platform(s) and thoroughly read the requirements for formatting, cover dimensions, and submission.
- **Acquire Necessary Software**
  Popular choices for writing and formatting include Microsoft Word, Google Docs, Scrivener, or Vellum (for Mac). Make sure your tool can output the correct file formats (PDF, EPUB, etc.).

---

5. Plan Your Launch

- **Pre-Launch Activities**
  - **Build an Email List**: Start collecting emails from potential readers or supporters.
  - **Create Buzz**: Share updates on social media, tease excerpts or cover reveals, and engage with online communities in your niche.
- **Launch Strategy**
  - **Coordinate Publication Dates**: Decide on a specific day (or window) to release your book.
  - **Gather Early Reviews**: Offer ARCs (Advance Reader Copies) or special previews to get initial feedback and social proof.
- **Post-Launch Promotions**
  - **Ongoing Marketing**: Schedule social media posts, run ads if budget allows, and reach out to influencers or bloggers in your genre.
  - **Track Results**: Monitor sales data and reviews, then adjust your approach as needed.

By following these five steps, you'll be well-positioned to bring your POD project from idea to reality. Whether you're launching a children's picture book, a how-to guide, or a novel, careful planning and organized execution will help you stand out in the competitive print-on-demand market. Good luck, and remember to adjust your plan as you learn more about your audience and your own creative process!

A Note of Gratitude

Thank you for taking the time to read through this guide and accompany me on this print-on-demand journey. Your support, curiosity, and dedication to learning have been the driving force behind every chapter. This book was crafted by **Joao Nsita**, and I hope it offers valuable insights and helps you take confident steps toward bringing your own publishing dreams to life. Keep pushing forward, embrace your creativity, and remember: the world of print on demand is filled with endless possibilities—yours to discover.

www.ingramcontent.com/pod-product-compliance
Lightning Source LLC
Chambersburg PA
CBHW050319230526
45471CB00005B/2254